Lakeboat

OTHER WORKS BY DAVID MAMET
PUBLISHED BY GROVE PRESS

American Buffalo
A Life in the Theatre
Reunion and *Dark Pony*
Sexual Perversity in Chicago and *The Duck Variations*
The Water Engine and *Mr. Happiness*
The Woods

Lakeboat

A PLAY BY David Mamet

GROVE PRESS, INC./NEW YORK

First Edition 1981
First Printing 1981
ISBN:0-394-51952-3
Library of Congress Catalog Card Number: 80-8919

First Evergreen Edition 1981
First Printing 1981
ISBN:0-394-17925-0
Library of Congress Catalog Card Number: 80-8919

Library of Congress Cataloging in Publication Data

Mamet, David.
    Lakeboat.

    I. Title.
PS3563.A4345L34   812'.54   80-8919
ISBN 0-394-51952-3   AACR2
ISBN 0-394-17925-0 (pbk.)

Manufactured in the United States of America

GROVE PRESS, INC., 196 West Houston Street, New York, N.Y. 10014

THIS PLAY IS DEDICATED
to John Dillon
and to Larry Shue.

Lakeboat was first staged by the Theatre Workshop at Marlboro College, Marlboro, Vermont, in 1970. It then sat in my trunk until John Dillon, Artistic Director of the Milwaukee Rep, discovered it in 1979.

John worked with me on the script, paring, arranging, and buttressing; and its present form is, in large part, thanks to him. I would also like to thank him and the men and women of the Milwaukee Rep—actors, designers, and crew—for their beautiful production of the play.

Lakeboat was first produced by the Court Street Theater, a project of the Milwaukee Repertory Theater, Milwaukee, Wisconsin, April 24, 1980, with the following cast:

PIERMAN	Gregory Leach
DALE	Thomas Hewitt
FIREMAN	Paul Meacham
STAN	Eugene J. Anthony
JOE	Larry Shue
COLLINS	John P. Connolly
SKIPPY	Robert Clites
FRED	Victor Raider-Wexler

This production was directed by John Dillon; settings by Laura Maurer; lighting by Rachel Budin, costumes by Colleen Muscha; properties by Sandy Struth; stage manager, Marcia Orbison.

Scene 1. What Do You Do With a Drunken Sailor?

Scene 2. Opening

Scene 3. Drink

Scene 4. Offloading

Scene 5. Fire and Evacuation Drills

Scene 6. The Illusion of Motion

Scene 7. The New Man

Scene 8. Woploving

Scene 9. Gauges

Scene 10. No Pussy

Scene 11. Mugged

Scene 12. Fred Busted at the Track

Scene 13. Fred on Horseracing

SCENE 14. Personal Sidearms

SCENE 15. The Cook Story

SCENE 16. Sidearms Continued

SCENE 17. Jonnie Fast

SCENE 18. The Inland Sea Around Us

SCENE 19. Arcana

SCENE 20. Dolomite

SCENE 21. The Bridge

SCENE 22. Fast Examined

SCENE 23. The .38

SCENE 24. Subterfuge

SCENE 25. Fingers

SCENE 26. Joe's Suicide

SCENE 27. Collins and Skippy on the Bridge

SCENE 28. In the Galley

The Characters

PIERMAN   30's or 40's.

DALE   Ordinary Seaman. 20.

FIREMAN   Engine. 60's.

STAN   Able-Bodied Seaman. Deck. 40's.

JOE   Able-Bodied Seaman. Deck. 40' or 50's.

COLLINS   Second Mate. 30's or 40's.

SKIPPY   First Mate. Late 50's.

FRED   Able-Bodied Seaman. Deck. 30's or 40's.

The Scene

The Lakeboat *T. Harrison.* The engine room,
the galley, the fantail (the farthest aft part of
the ship), the boat deck, the rail.

The set, I think, should be a *construction* of
a Lakeboat, so that all playing areas can be seen
at once, no scenery needs to be shifted, and the
actors can simply walk from one area to the
next as their scenes require.

Scene 1
What Do You Do With a Drunken Sailor?

The Lakeboat is being offloaded. DALE *talks with the* PIERMAN, *who is supervising the offloading.*

PIERMAN: Did you hear about Skippy and the new kid?

DALE: What new kid?

PIERMAN: Night cook. Whatsisname that got mugged?

DALE: No. What happened?

PIERMAN: Well, you know, this new kid is on the beach . . .

DALE: Yeah. . . .

PIERMAN: And, how it happened, he's in East Chicago after the last pay draw . . .

DALE: Yeah. . . .

PIERMAN: . . . last week and drawed all he could and he's making the bars with a C or so in his pocket and flashing the wad every chance he gets. . . .

DALE: Oh boy.

PIERMAN: What does the kid know? What do they know at that age, no offense.

DALE: Yeah.

PIERMAN: And, as I understand it, this slut comes on to him, and they leave the bar and he gets rolled.

DALE: By the whore?

PIERMAN: Yeah, I mean he'd had a few . . .

DALE: The bitch.

PIERMAN: . . . and wasn't in any shape. Anyway she takes his wad and his Z card.

DALE: Not his Z card?

PIERMAN: Yep and his gate pass. . . .

DALE: And he didn't even get laid . . . did he?

PIERMAN: Fuck no, she rolled him first. Then she left.

DALE: Bitch.

PIERMAN: So, he stumbles back to the gate, drunk and sobbing. . . .

DALE: Nothing to be ashamed of. . . .

PIERMAN: The guards won't let him in! I mean he's bleeding, he's dirty. . . .

DALE: You didn't tell me he was bleeding.

PIERMAN: It was understood. . . .

DALE: So, go on.

PIERMAN: And dirty, and no identification. So, of course, they won't let him in.

DALE: Bastards.

PIERMAN: Yeah, well, they're just doing their job.

DALE: I suppose you're right.

PIERMAN: Pretty nice guys, actually.

DALE: I suppose.

PIERMAN: And so . . . where was I?

DALE: The part where they won't let him in.

PIERMAN: And so the guards won't let him in. But, uh

... whatsisname, guy about thirty, so, you know him?

DALE: I'm new.

PIERMAN: Well, whatsisname happens to be coming through and of course he recognizes . . . whatsisname.

DALE: Yeah.

PIERMAN: So, "What happened? Are you all right?" . . . all that shit. And the guard explains to him how they can't let the guy through and the guy vouches right up for him.

DALE: He's a good man, huh?

PIERMAN: And they *still* won't let him through.

DALE: Yeah.

PIERMAN: So, how he got *in* . . .

DALE: Yeah.

PIERMAN: He waited until these guards are looking the other way . . .

DALE: Yeah.

PIERMAN: . . . at a secretary or a train, I don't know. And they walked right through the main gate.

DALE: Bunch of assholes, huh?

PIERMAN: Well, I don't know. . . . So, what happened with Skippy . . . you know Skippy?

DALE: No.

PIERMAN: The First Mate.

Pause.

DALE: Oh yeah.

PIERMAN: So what happened with him is this: The poor slob gets back to the fucking boat—drunk and bleeding and broke, right?

DALE: Poor sonofabitch.

PIERMAN: He gets to the gangway and the second is on deck supervising offloading.

DALE: Right.

PIERMAN: Talking on the box with Skippy, the First Mate, who is up in the bridge. Now, Skippy sees this poor thing tromping up the pier and he says to Collins, the second, "Collins, we got passengers this trip," which they did, "Get that man below and tell him to stay there until he's sober."

DALE: Huh.

PIERMAN: Although he is a hell of a nice guy, Skippy. Oldest First Mate on the Lakes. Did you know that?

DALE: No.

PIERMAN: Was a Master once. I don't know who for. That's why they call him Skippy.

DALE: How do you know that?

PIERMAN: I heard it. I don't actually know it. But that's why they call him Skippy. And so, anyway, Collins collars the slob and tells him to get below. "Who says so?" the guy says. "The First says so," Collins says. Guigliani, Guilini, something like that.

DALE: What?

PIERMAN: The guy's name. So anyway. Guigliani, whatsisname, says, "Tell the First to go fuck himself."

DALE: Oh, Christ.

PIERMAN: So, as God would have it, at that precise moment the box rings and it's Skippy wanting to talk to Collins. "Collins," he says, "What's holding up the Number Three Hold?" "I'm talking to Guliami," says Collins. "What the all-fired fuck does he have to say that is so important?" says Skippy. "He's telling me I should tell you to go fuck yourself. . . ." says Collins. So Skippy, who bandied enough words at this point, says, "Collins, throw that man in the canal and get Three Hold the fuck offloaded," which I was working on, too, at that point.

DALE: So?

PIERMAN: So what?

DALE: So did he throw him in the canal?

PIERMAN: I don't know, I was below. I *heard* this.

Pause.

DALE: And where is the guy now?

PIERMAN: What am I, a mindreader? On the beach somewhere, lost his job. Up in East Chicago, I guess.

DALE: Poor sonofabitch.

PIERMAN: Oh, I don't know.

The PIERMAN *goes on board the boat.*

Scene 2
Opening

DALE *talks to the audience.* STAN *is on the boat. The* FIREMAN *comes up the gangplank, followed by* JOE.

DALE *(to audience):* That's the Lakeboat. Built 1938 for Czerwiecki Steel. Christened *Joseph Czerwiecki.* Sold to Harrison Steel, East Chicago, Indiana, 1954, renamed *T. Harrison.* Length overall 615 feet. Depth 321 feet. Keel 586 feet. Beam 60. The floating home of 45 men.

FIREMAN: Guigliani got mugged.

DALE: I'm his replacement. Gross tons 8,225. Capacity in tons 11,406. A fair-sized boat. A small world . . .

FIREMAN: So I've heard.

JOE *comes on board.*

STAN: Yo, Joe.

JOE: Hiya.

DALE: . . . *T. Harrison.* A steel bulk-freight turbine steamer registered in the Iron Ore Trade.

STAN: You pick up those razor blades?

JOE: Shit. I fucking forgot, I'm sorry.

Scene 3
Drink

A conversation on the fantail. STAN *and* JOE *are killing time while the boat is at the pier.*

STAN: Boy was I drunk last night.

JOE: I'm still drunk.

STAN: That wine. Drink wine and it dehydrates you. When you drink water the next morning it activates the alcohol.

JOE: I'm so hung over I can't see.

STAN: Can't see, I can't even talk.

JOE: I can't even fucking think straight.

STAN: You couldn't think straight last night.

JOE: I was drunk last night.

STAN: You're still drunk.

JOE: Yep.

STAN: No good, man.

JOE: Yep.

STAN: No damn good.

JOE: Sure not.

STAN: No fucking good.

JOE: What? . . . Drinking?

STAN: Drinking, life, women, the Boat. No good.

JOE: It's not that bad.

STAN: No fuckin' good.

JOE: You been drinking?

STAN: Drinking? Don't talk to me about drinking. What the hell did it ever get me? Drinking? I was drinking before you were wiping your own ass. Beer? I've drunk more beer in my time than I can remember. I could tick off my life in beer caps. Bottles, cans, pop-tops, screw-tops, bottles . . . every man on the ship had his own opener.

JOE: I remember.

STAN: Around the neck. Holy Mary. Don't tell me

about beer, Joe. Please don't tell me about
beer. Domestic and imported. Beer? I've drunk
beer. . . . Wine!

JOE: Ah, wine.

STAN: Used to drink it with every meal. White, cherry.
Love the stuff. You need a taste for wine.

JOE: I've got one.

STAN: Domestic and imported.

JOE: I love the stuff.

STAN: Red and *white.* I've drunk it. Wine with my food,
cigarettes smoldering and chilled wine. Wine with
fruit. Warmed, spice wine. Sweet cherry wine. I
know wine, Joe.

JOE: What about liquors?

STAN: What about them?

JOE: Yeah.

STAN: For faggots. But booze . . .

JOE: Booze!

STAN: Scotch and rye. Drink bourbon by the fifth.
When I lived at home? Drink? My father could
drink.

JOE: My father could, too.

STAN: I say that man could put it *away*. A fifth a day and more, Joe, and *more*.

JOE: My father, too.

STAN: He loved the stuff.

JOE: It killed him, my father.

STAN: Drink it by the fifth. He never lacked for booze, that man. That's one thing I can say for him.

JOE: Yeah.

STAN: Nothing too good for him.

JOE: Yeah.

STAN: The old fart'd drink Sterno. He didn't give a shit.

JOE: I know.

STAN: That man could *drink*.

JOE: What about your mother?

STAN: She could drink, too.

JOE: My mother couldn't drink.

STAN: No?

JOE: Old man said it was bad for her.

STAN: What do they know of booze, the cunts?

JOE: Nothing.

STAN: They can't drink. You ever know a woman who could drink?

JOE: Yeah.

STAN: What do they know?

JOE: A girl in Duluth.

STAN: They don't understand it. It's a man's thing, drinking. A curse and an elevation. Makes you an angel. A booze-ridden angel. Drinking? I know my alcohol, boyo. I know it and you know I know it. And I know it.

JOE: I'll take you below. I gotta go on watch.

STAN: Domestic and imported.

JOE: Come on, Stan.

STAN: Any way you call it.

JOE: I gotta go on watch.

STAN: Mixed drinks? I know my mixed drinks. You name one, I know it. Mixed drinks.

JOE: . . . Manhattan.

STAN: I know it.

JOE: Come on, Stan.

STAN: Ah, leave me alone.

JOE: Come on, I gotta go on watch.

STAN: So go on watch, you fucking Polack.

JOE: Who's a Polack?

STAN: Trust a Polack . . . to go on watch . . . when I'm pissed.

JOE: I'll take you down to the dunnage room and get you some coffee.

STAN: Don't want any coffee. Want to go to sleep.

JOE: Well, let's go, then.

STAN: I want to sleep by myself.

JOE: Okay, Stan, let's get you off your feet.

STAN: Offa deck.

JOE: Sure.

STAN: And who are you to tell me to get off the deck of a ship we both happen to be on?

JOE: Come on, goddamnit.

STAN: Getting mad, huh?

JOE: Stosh.

STAN: Getting a trifle warm. Aren't you getting warm?

JOE: Okay, Stan.

STAN: Fucking no-class Polack.

JOE: Okay Stan.

STAN: Can't even hold your liquor.

JOE *walks off.*

Scene 4
Offloading

JOE *wanders into the galley.* COLLINS *finds him there and puts him to work.*

COLLINS: Litko!

JOE: Yo!

COLLINS: Skippy wants a sandwich.

JOE: . . . I just came on.

COLLINS: Get him a sandwich, will you?

JOE: I just came *on.* . . .

COLLINS: It'll take you a minute.

JOE: Uh.

COLLINS: *Huh?*

JOE: What about the nightman?

COLLINS: He got mugged.

JOE: Yeah? By who?

COLLINS: Now, how the fuck should I know?

JOE: You got a cigarette?

   Pause.

COLLINS: Yeah.

JOE: Thanks.

   PIERMAN *enters galley.*

PIERMAN: Hot.

COLLINS: Can we speed this up at all?

PIERMAN: You'll be out by about two.

COLLINS: You think?

PIERMAN: Two, three. Got time for a cup?

COLLINS: Yeah. Joe, go see what kind of sandwich Skippy wants, huh?

JOE: Yeah. *(Exits.)*

PIERMAN: Any chance of something to eat?

COLLINS: Lost the nightman.

PIERMAN: Oh yeah. . . . Sorry.

COLLINS (*pause*): Cook's up the street. (*Pause.*) You want some pie?

PIERMAN: Yeah.

COLLINS: Any special kind?

PIERMAN: Yeah, blueberry. What you got?

COLLINS: We got some.

PIERMAN: It's a bitch in here.

COLLINS: Yeah.

PIERMAN: Cooler on the dock.

COLLINS: Yeah.

PIERMAN: What's the next trip, Arthur?

COLLINS: Duluth.

PIERMAN: Yeah? Cool up there.

JOE *enters.*

COLLINS (*to* JOE): What'd he want?

JOE: Egg on white bread.

PIERMAN: Any guys on break out there, you notice?

JOE: I didn't notice.

PIERMAN: Uh.

JOE: I was thinking about my sandwich. We gonna have a new nightman, Mr. Collins?

COLLINS: Huh?

JOE: Nightman.

COLLINS: Yeah, sure. Crender said we'll have him this trip.

JOE: That's good. I don't want to make these sandwiches all the way to Canada. If you know what I mean. Not that I mind it. I just fucking hate making sandwiches. For other people to eat.

COLLINS: Don't worry.

JOE: I don't mind cooking for myself, though.

COLLINS: Wrap it in wax paper, will you?

JOE: Yeah, sure.

COLLINS (*leaving the galley*): And make sure you get those boats clean today, huh?

JOE: Right as rain.

Scene 5
Fire and Evacuation Drills

SKIPPY, *making a tour of the boat, runs into* DALE.

SKIPPY: That's right, assholes. Fuck off on your fire and evacuation drills and your ass is going to be in a big sling when we have to drill for the Coast Guard. You!

DALE: Yes sir.

SKIPPY: What's your number?

DALE: What number, sir?

SKIPPY: F and E. *(Pause.)* F and E, boy—

DALE: I don't know what that means, sir.

SKIPPY: Fire. Fire and evacuation.

DALE: I . . . don't think I have one.

SKIPPY: How long have you been on this ship?

DALE: About three minutes, sir.

SKIPPY: Yeah. Well, check out your fire and evacuation number, for God's sake, will you? Your F and E number, will you?

DALE: Yessir. Who do I check it out with?

SKIPPY: I do not know. Ask Joe Litko. You know him?

DALE: I can find him, sir.

SKIPPY: Good *for* you. Well, find him and listen hard.

DALE: Yessir.

SKIPPY: Bunch of children.

Scene 6
The Illusion of Motion

SKIPPY *continues back to the bridge, where he finds* COLLINS.

SKIPPY: Where's my sandwich?

COLLINS: Litko's getting it.

SKIPPY: He's not in Stewards. Where's the nightman?

COLLINS: Got mugged. He's in the hospital.

SKIPPY: What's the number in Stewards?

COLLINS: 2—3.

SKIPPY: Call for me on that sandwich.

COLLINS *(on the intercom):* Stewards? Collins calling on that sandwich for Skippy. Well, who is there? Where's Litko? Well, get him.

Pause.

This is Collins, Second . . . *(to* SKIPPY*)* they hung up. *(He spies* LITKO *on the deck.)* There's Litko. LITKO! GO PICK UP THE DECK PHONE. NO! DON'T COME HERE, PICK UP THE PHONE.

STAN *and* FRED *passing by.*

STAN: This boat is becoming a bureaucracy.

FRED: Tell me.

They continue off. Phone rings.

COLLINS *(into phone):* Bridge, Collins. Litko, I've been trying to get you. What the fuck happened on Skippy's egg? Where have you been? Boatdeck? What about that sandwich. *(to* SKIPPY*)* New Nightman showed up.

SKIPPY: Book him. Forget Litko.

COLLINS *(into phone):* Litko, forget it. Go back to the boats. Yeah. No. Forget it. *(He hangs up.)*

SKIPPY: What's he doing on the boatdeck?

COLLINS: Reading.

SKIPPY: What's he reading? See if you can find out.

STAN *and* FRED *stroll off.*

STAN *(to* FRED): Who was the most grotesque girl you ever fucked?

FRED: I'd have to think about that.

SKIPPY: I'd like to know.

Scene 7
The New Man

COLLINS *returns to the galley and encounters* DALE.

COLLINS: You the new man?

DALE: I guess.

COLLINS: You're going to be the new nightman. Night-cook. You ever cooked before?

DALE: No, a little.

COLLINS: Well, we're going to book you nightman, what's your name?

DALE: Katzman, Dale.

COLLINS: All right. We're going to book you. Then you're off until 10 P.M. tonight. You work ten till six-thirty straight shift. Half-hour for lunch. Your work should take you about four, five hours.

Phone rings.

Get that.

DALE: Hello, kitchen. Wait a minute. He wants the Mate.

COLLINS: Gimme that. Collins. Yo. They're off. He got mugged. We got one. What kind? Fuck you. Okay. *(To* DALE*)* You know how to make a sandwich?

DALE: Sure.

COLLINS: Make one for the First. The First Mate. And then make one for the Fireman.

DALE: Right. What kind?

COLLINS: For the First, an egg . . . and for the Fireman, how the fuck should I know? Make him an egg. All right?

DALE: Sure.

COLLINS: Good.

Scene 8
Woploving

The FIREMAN, JOE, *and* STAN *are shooting the breeze in the engine room.*

FIREMAN: So, the way I hear it: she told him she was divorced. How about that.

JOE: So what?

FIREMAN: I'm divorced.

JOE: Sorry.

FIREMAN: So they started to get really blind.

JOE: My mother is blind.

Pause.

FIREMAN: And could he spare her some change, twenty for the kids, a saw for some groceries, you know.

JOE: Yeah.

FIREMAN: And all of the time she's drinking this rum with coke and lime.

JOE: Coke *and* lime?

FIREMAN: That's what I heard.

JOE: That's how they drink it in Italy.

FIREMAN: You never been to Italy.

JOE: Now how the FUCK do you know?

FIREMAN: I . . .

JOE: How the everlasting cocksucking FUCK do you know I never been to Italy?

FIREMAN: Jesus.

JOE: Don't do shit all day and tells me where I never been. *(Exits.)*

FIREMAN *(to* STAN*)*: So, Collins tells me, she'd have a drink . . .

STAN: Yeah.

FIREMAN: He'd have a drink.

STAN: Yeah.

FIREMAN: But pretty soon he's getting up knocking

over tables and he's staggering ready to die and
she's walking in a straight line. Say, I wonder
what's the matter with Joe?

STAN: Why do you say something's the matter with
him?

FIREMAN: I only . . .

STAN: Who the hell are you?

FIREMAN: I only meant . . .

STAN: Twenty-some years on the boats watching a little
dial and you know about what's "wrong with
Joe?"

FIREMAN: Lookit . . .

STAN: Just listen to me. The man has done more shit in
his life than you'll ever *forget*.

FIREMAN: I only said.

STAN: Just remember that, Mr. Wiseass. He's been
more places in his life than you *ever* been.

FIREMAN: He's never been to Italy.

STAN: What kind of woploving bullshit is that?

FIREMAN: *I'm* fucking Italian, don't talk to *me*, Fred.

DALE (*enters the engine room. Generally*): Hi.

STAN: Hi.

Pause.

DALE: How are you?

STAN: Fine.

DALE: That's good.

STAN: In the sense that I feel like shit. Been to Italy. (*He exits.*)

DALE: You want a sandwich?

FIREMAN: Yeah. You the new nightman?

DALE: Yes. Do you like egg?

FIREMAN: I don't give a fuck.

Scene 9
Gauges

DALE: What do you do down here?

FIREMAN: Down here? I read.

DALE: How can you read and do your job?

FIREMAN: I'm not answerable to you. I'm answerable to the Chief.

DALE: I was just asking.

FIREMAN: I do my job okay.

DALE: I know that.

FIREMAN: I do it okay. I keep busy. . . . I read a bit. . . .

DALE: It doesn't get in your way, the reading?

FIREMAN: Nooo. I mean, I gotta watch the two gauges. Four actually. We got the two main, they're the two you gotta watch, and the two auxiliary.

DALE: Uh huh.

FIREMAN: But you gotta keep your eye on those two main, because if they go, well . . .

DALE: *Oh*, yeah.

FIREMAN: I mean if that main goes, if she goes redline, you're fucking fucked.

DALE: You switch over to the auxiliary?

FIREMAN: I don't do nothing! I don't do a damn nothing. I'm not supposed to touch a thing. I shut down whichever blows, larboard or starboard. I shut down and I call the bridge and I call in the Chief, in that order.

DALE: And then you watch the auxiliary?

FIREMAN: Nothing to watch. The engine's shut down and the gauges is dead.

DALE: Well, what's the point of having an auxiliary gauge?

FIREMAN: For a standby. You gotta have a standby. . . .

DALE: Oh.

FIREMAN: You don't have a standby, with that automatic oil feed! You don't have a standby and the

main goes, you're fucking *fucked.* You know what
I mean.

DALE: Oh yeah.

Pause.

And you keep an eye on them, huh?

FIREMAN: What do you mean, "keep an eye on them?"
I'm watching 'em constantly. That's my job.

DALE: I see that.

FIREMAN: Of course, I read a *bit.* I mean, when you get
down to it. What is there to do? Watching two
gauges for four hours a clip?

DALE: Uh huh.

FIREMAN: That's eight hours a day watching two
gauges. If you don't read, do something, you'd go
insane.

Scene 10
No Pussy

DALE *climbs up out of the engine room and is accosted by* FRED.

FRED: You the new man?

DALE: Yep. Dale. Dale Katzman.

FRED: Jewish, huh?

DALE: Yeah.

FRED: No offense.

DALE: Thanks.

Pause.

FRED: Well, Dale . . . Coming on like this out of nowhere you got a thing or two to find out. Now, the main thing about the boats, other than their primary importance in the Steel Industry, is that you don't get any pussy. You got that?

DALE: Yes.

FRED: Except when we tie up. This is important to know because it precludes your whole life on the boats. This is why everyone says "fuck" all the time.

DALE: Why?

FRED: They say "fuck" in direct proportion to how bored they are. Huh?

DALE: Yeah.

FRED: Now, from the prospect of not getting any . . . you know about sex?

DALE: I know it all.

FRED: I see you mean that facetiously.

DALE: Yeah.

FRED: Because there sure is a hell of a lot to find out. I'm not going to offend you, am I?

DALE: I don't know.

FRED: Okay.

Pause.

You know, I didn't find out about sex until late in

life, judging from my age of puberty, you gotta go on watch?

DALE: Not until ten.

FRED: . . . which came quite early, who can say why? Huh?

DALE: Yeah.

FRED: Around eight. What did I know then, right? Stroke books, jacking off with a few choice friends, you know. Am I right?

DALE: You're right.

FRED: For *years*. Until I'm in high school and I fall for this girl. Same old story, right? She's beautiful, she's smart, and I dig her. I take her out, right? So, times are different then (this was a few years ago) and after the movies we're dryhumping in the living room. The father is asleep upstairs, the mother is dead, same old story, right?

DALE: Right.

FRED: And all of a sudden the whole thing becomes clear to me. I mean in a flash all this horseshit about the Universe becomes clear to me, and I perceive meaning in life: I WANT TO FUCK. I want to stick it inside of her. Screw dryhumping. I want to get it wet. I want to become one with the ages of men and women before me down into eternity and goo in the muck from whence we sprung . . . you know what I mean?

DALE: I know.

FRED: And I'm on fire. I'm going OOOOOOOOOoh and AAAAAAAAAAAAaaah and like that and trying to undo her brassiere. (This girl had tits.) I don't even bother anymore. You know what I say? "You do it," I say. The joy is gone, you know? So, anyway. We're still humping and bumping and I'm trying to undo the brassiere and my knee, as if it had a mind of its own, and never a word spoken, had inserted itself between her legs and she's gyrating like crazy and saying . . . What do you think she is saying?

DALE: "I love you?"

FRED: "No," she is saying, "Oh, Fred, please don't."

DALE: So?

FRED: So, like a dope, I don't. We look sheepish for a minute. She gets all straightened out and says she had a wonderful time, Freddy, and out I go. So, to make a long story short, after this happened another time, two times, I begin to get wise something is not as it should be. Also I can't walk in the mornings. But my uncle, who is over, is conversing with me one night and, as men will do, we start talking about sex. He tells a story, I tell *My* story. This takes him aback. "What?" he says. "The way to get laid is to treat them like shit." Now, you just stop for a moment and think on that. You've heard it before and you'll hear it again but there is more to it than meets the eye. Listen: THE WAY TO GET LAID IS TO TREAT THEM LIKE SHIT. Truer words have never been spoken. And this has been tested by better men than you or me. *So,* I thought it out a bit and decided to put it into action. I'm going out with Janice. Movies, walk home, couch, dryhumping, no . . . I hit her in the mouth. I don't mean slap, Dale, this is important. I mean hit, I fucking pasted her. She didn't know nothing. She is so surprised she didn't even bleed. Not a word did I speak, but off with her dress, panties, and my pants. I didn't wear any underwear. A lot of women find that attractive, did you know that?

DALE: No.

FRED: Well, I've only since found that out. Anyway. Smacko, spread the old chops and I humped the shit out of her. She's yelling: OOOOh. Don't, OOOOH, yessssssss, OOOOooooh don't, Freddy, Yes, it's so gooooooooood, my father'll hear oooooooh. SHEEEEEEEEEEEEIT. Zingo. So I got dressed and she's lying there on the couch spent, I mean, spent and wet and everything. (She looked beautiful.) And I go over to the door. "Not another word out of you, cunt," I say. "Ever."

DALE: What about her father?

FRED: He was a boilermaker. So. After that it's hand-jobs in the assembly hall, fucking under the bleachers, the whole thing, man. She's buying presents and asking *me* to the prom (I'd left school). And to this day. I mean to this day, I want a piece, I call her up and tell her, not ask her, *tell* Daley, I tell her where and when, and she's there. And she's *married.* So remember. . . . I know, I *know*, I was a shy kid *too*. But you gotta remember, the way to a woman's cunt is right through her cunt. That's the only way. *Fershtay?*

DALE: Uh huh.

FRED: Let's get something to eat.

DALE: I gotta make up the First's cabin.

FRED: Okay. I'm gonna see you later.

JOE *and* STAN *pass. We hear part of their conversation.*

JOE: Guy can't take care of himself he oughta stay out of East Chicago. *Huh?*

STAN: Yeah.

Pause.

JOE: They aren't in business for their health. . . .

Scene 11
Mugged

FRED, *alone by the rail, soliloquizes.*

FRED: Mugged. Yeah. Poor son of bitch. In East Chicago. That's a lousy town. By some whore, no less. Drugged the shit out of him, I guess. Met her in a bar. Who knows. He was a fanatic, you know? I knew him. Not overly well, but I knew him. He was a gambling degenerate. Played the ponies. How did he do I don't know. But I had my suspicions that he gave it all away. So who knows. Maybe the Maf got him. I mean, somebody got him. Maybe the whore, huh? So maybe it's the Murphy man, but I don't think so. It looks like the Outfit. Not that they care for the few C's they took. But you know how they are. You can't get behind. When you're into them that's it. Am I right? No. It doesn't figure. Unless it was the Outfit. Or some freak occurrence. It was probably some Outfit guys got him. Assuming he was into them. It doesn't look like he just got rolled. Beat the living fuck out of him. Left him for dead. Huh? Can you feature it? Flies in his face. Fuck-

ing ear stuck to the sidewalk with blood. Rup-
tured man, he'll never perform again. Ribs, back.
The *back*. Hit him in the back. Left him for *dead*.

Pause.

It doesn't figure. The only way it adds up, if it was
the Outfit. A very property-oriented group. Poor
sucker.

Scene 12
Fred Busted at the Track

FRED *wanders into the galley, where he meets* STAN.

STAN: Boy, did I get laid last night.

FRED: One of the guys on the boat?

STAN: By a woman, Freddie, a woman. You remember them? Soft things with a hole in the middle.

FRED: I remember them.

STAN: You look down, Freddy.

FRED: I am down.

Pause.

Why did they have to go and build a racetrack on the South Side of Chicago?

STAN: Somebody made a survey. What did you lose?

FRED: Seven hundred bucks.

STAN: Where'd you get seven hundred bucks?

FRED: Around.

STAN: Oh.

> *Pause.*

> You in trouble?

FRED: No.

STAN: You sure?

FRED: Yeah.

> *Pause.*

STAN: You sure?

FRED: Yeah. Thank you. Yeah.

STAN: You'd tell me if you were?

FRED: Yeah.

> *Pause.*

STAN: Okay you watch yourself.

> STAN *leaves the galley.*

FRED: Thank you.

Scene 13
Fred on Horseracing

FRED *continues his soliloquy.*

FRED: Because it's clean. The track is clean. It's like life without all the complicating people. At the track there are no two ways. There is win, place, show, and out-of-the-money. You decide, you're set. I mean, how clean can you get? Your bet is down and it's DOWN. And the winners always pay. Something. Into the turn, backstretch, spinning into the turn and heading for home. It's poetry. It's a computer. You don't even have to look at the fucking things. It's up on the board and it's final and there are two types of people in the world.

Pause.

Next post in fifteen minutes.

COLLINS *(entering the galley):* The next post is up your ass if you don't get to work.

FRED: I'm gone.

FRED *leaves the galley and runs into* JOE *on the deck.*

JOE: *(as if resuming a conversation):* . . . why I never got along with women. I just had too much dynamite in me.

FRED: . . . it happens. . . .

They walk down the fantail.

Scene 14
Personal Sidearms

SKIPPY *and* COLLINS *are on the bridge.*

SKIPPY: . . . the *Luger* was the enlisted man's sidearm, and the *Walther* was the officer's.

COLLINS: Are you sure?

SKIPPY: I was *there,* my friend. I was *there.* . . .

Scene 15
The Cook Story

JOE *and* FRED *on the fantail.*

FRED: I heard the cook has two Cadillac Eldorados.

JOE: This year's?

FRED: Last year. One in Chicago, Chicago Harbor, and the other in Arthur.

JOE: How long's he been on the run?

FRED: About twenty years, I guess.

JOE: Yeah.

FRED: More or less . . . ten, twenty years.

JOE: What's he want with two Caddies?

FRED: So's he can have one here and one there.

JOE: So he can have one everywhere he goes.

FRED: Yeah. Well, he's only got two. He's not married.

JOE: That's it. That's the big difference. Right?

FRED: You said it. That's the difference . . . between him . . .

JOE: Yeah, that's it. Cocksucker can probably *afford* two cars.

FRED: Oh, yeah. Well, he's got 'em.

JOE: Cocksucker probably doesn't know what it *is* to be married.

FRED: He was married once.

JOE: Yeah?

FRED: Yeah, I think. Yeah. He was married. I heard that.

JOE: Where'd you hear it, on the Boat?

FRED: Yeah. He used to be married. To a girl. She used to ship on the Boats.

JOE: Yeah?

FRED: Oh yeah, they used to ship Stewards together. They stopped. They got divorced.

JOE: Bastard's probably forgot what it is to be married.

Pause.

Two cars.

FRED: What the fuck? He worked for them.

JOE: I'm not saying he didn't work for them.

FRED: Oh no.

JOE: I never said that, I mean, it's obvious he worked
for them. He's got 'em, right?

FRED: As far as I know.

JOE: Well, has he got 'em or not?

FRED: Yeah, he's got 'em . . . as far as I know.

JOE: Probably only got a couple of Chevys.

FRED: Yeah.

JOE: A couple of '56 Chevys.

FRED: Yeah.

JOE: Cocksucker's only probably got a pair of used
Volkswagens.

FRED: I don't know. . . .

JOE: Or a beat-up Buick.

FRED: Yeah.

JOE: Or a fucking De*Soto* for Christ's sake. Who the fuck knows he's got two Caddies?

FRED: Well, he's not married. I know that much.

JOE: Lucky son of a bitch.

FRED: It's a tough life.

JOE: Oh yeah?

FRED: Yeah. I was married once.

JOE: Yeah?

FRED: Yeah. I'm still married. To my second wife.

JOE: You got divorced, huh?

FRED: Why do you say that?

JOE: You just said you're married to your second wife.

FRED: Oh yeah. I got divorced . . . from my first.

JOE: Yeah, I'm sorry. I mean, she could of died. You could of been a widower.

FRED: It's too late now.

JOE: You pay any alimony?

FRED: Yeah, ho, shit, did I pay? I was doing extra deck-work and running to the track so that woman could fuck off and pamper the kids.

JOE: How many kids you have?

FRED: . . . just one, actually. I don't know why I said "kids."

JOE: They live with their mother, huh?

FRED: Yeah. Actually there's just one kid, Clarice. She's the kid.

JOE: A girl, huh?

FRED: Yeah. She lives with her mother.

JOE: You see her?

FRED: Oh yeah. What do you think? I just let her live with that cunt? Christ. I see her every chance I get. Her birthday . . . we go to the *zoo* . . . museums. . . . She got married, my wife, ex.

JOE: Well, shit. At least you don't have to pay alimony.

FRED: Yeah. But doesn't she fuck me on the child support? Every fucking piece of kleenex has to come from Carson Pirie Scott. What fucking kid spends eighty dollars a month? What happens to eighty dollars a month? I'll tell you, Denise ex-fucking-Swoboda is what happens. Nothing is too good for the kid. But it takes a bite.

JOE: What doesn't?

FRED: That is a point, Joe. It's getting expensive just to live.

JOE: Sure as shit.

FRED: Just to buy a pack of Camels is getting you have to go to the fucking bank. Used to be twenty-six cents a pack in Indiana.

JOE: I can remember it used to be seventeen cents in Tennessee.

FRED: You aren't from there.

JOE: We used to go there.

FRED: Ah.

JOE *(pause):* I wish I never got started. I used to buy 'em for my old man. He used to say, "You gotta smoke, don't hide it. Smoke in my presence."

FRED: So did you?

JOE: Christ no, he woulda beat the shit outta me.

FRED: You should never of gotten started. It's too fuck-ing expensive. Fuck. Eighty-five cents.

JOE: It's going up.

FRED: Where is it going to stop? I swear to God I don't

know. We'll all be selling syphilitic fucking apples to each other on the street corner.

JOE: You give any money on Poppyseed days?

FRED: No. They want loot, let 'em work on the ship.

JOE: I always wanted to be a pirate. Ever since I was a little kid.

FRED: . . . or digging ditches, though somebody's gotta run the ships, right?

JOE: . . . yeah.

FRED: I mean, the cook's gotta keep up his payments.

JOE: That's a good one, all right.

Scene 16
Sidearms Continued

On the bridge.

COLLINS: So what was the Walther Luger.

SKIPPY: There was no such thing.

COLLINS: I read it.

SKIPPY: Where?

COLLINS: In some book on the War.

SKIPPY: Then you were lied to. There was no such thing. Believe me.

Pause.

COLLINS: I *read* it.

SKIPPY: No. I'd tell you if it were the case. *(Pause.)* I would. If it were the case.

Scene 17
Jonnie Fast

FRED *and* STAN *are smoking cigarettes on the boat deck.*

FRED: I'm going to *tell* you: Jonnie Fast is the strongest guy in ten years.

STAN: You know what? You are truly an idiot. You could of said that in the dark and I would of known it was you because only you could make so stupid a statement. Jonnie Fast has got to be the dumbest cocksucker I can remember.

FRED: Yeah. That's like you to say that.

STAN: You know about it . . . ?

FRED: I know when a guy is strong.

STAN: And that's what Fast is. Strong, huh?

FRED: Yeah.

STAN: You know. I agree with you one hundred percent. He is strong, this Fast. He's probably the strongest guy I've ever seen. I can't think of anything that would be stronger than he is. Unless maybe a pile of shit.

FRED: What do you know. Who do you like?

STAN: Oh . . . I'll tell you. You want a really *strong* fellow. A real type, I'd have to say . . . Jerry Lewis. He could probably knock the shit outta Fast.

FRED: You don't know nothing. You don't know a champ when you're fucking looking at him at the movies, for chrissake. This guy is stark. He is the best.

STAN: He's the best, all right. Like jacking off is better than getting laid. This guy Fast is the fucking jackoff of all time.

FRED: Yeah. I see your point, Stan. I agree with you. The man is not stark. He's no fucking good. That's why he didn't take five fucking guys in that barroom using only one pool cue. I see your point.

STAN: Shirley Temple probably couldn't've taken those guys, I suppose.

FRED: Oh, no. Shirley Temple probably could've taken them. She could've disarmed them and probably shot that meat knife out've the guy's hand from twenty feet from the hip . . . yeah, I see your point.

STAN: And I suppose this guy could whip the shit out've Clint Eastwood, huh? I really think that. Explain that to me, will you, Joe? How Clint Eastwood is no match for this guy?

FRED: Oh, well . . .

STAN: No, explain it to me.

FRED: If you want to get ridiculous about it . . .

STAN: Or Lee Van Cleef. I'm *sure*, he would've laid down and puked from fear when he saw this guy two blocks off.

FRED: All I know is, like you say, any guy who fucks all night and drinks a shitload of champagne and can go out at five the next morning and rob a bank without a hitch has to be no fucking good. I see your point.

STAN: "No fucking good?" No! He's great! He only had the entire National Guard worth of sidekicks, about two thousand guys and an A-bomb to back him up. You really gotta admire a stand-up guy like that.

FRED: He didn't have no bomb.

STAN: Pardon me.

FRED: Where do you get this "bomb" shit? You probably didn't even see the movie, all you know.

STAN: No, you're right. I probably didn't even see the movie. That's how come I don't know what a bustout Jonnie Fast is, and what a complete loser you are to back him. I probably never did see the picture. In fact, I've probably never been to a movie in my life and I'm not standing on a boat. And your name isn't Fred, I suppose. Oh, and you're probably not completely full of shit.

FRED: Probably not.

STAN: You idiot, what do you know.

STAN *walks off.*

Scene 18
The Inland Sea Around Us

JOE, *on the boat deck, is contemplating the lake.* COL-
LINS, *making his evening rounds, walks by.*

JOE: Evening, Mr. Collins.

COLLINS: Joe.

JOE: Mr. Collins, how far is it to land out here?

COLLINS: I don't know, about five miles.

JOE: How long could a guy live out here, do you think?

COLLINS: What?

JOE: I mean, not if he was on an island or anything, or
in a boat. I mean in the water. I mean . . . it's over
your head.

COLLINS: Don't really know, Joe. You planning a swim?

JOE: Swim? Swim? Oh! I get you. A swim! Yeah, no. I

was just wondering in case, God forbid, we should go down and the lifeboats were all leaky or something. How long do you think a fellow would last?

COLLINS: Joe . . .

JOE: You can tell me.

COLLINS: Don't worry about it, huh? Even if the boat sunk you've got jackets and they'd have a helicopter here in a half-hour.

JOE: Oh, I don't worry about it. I just wonder. You know.

COLLINS: Sure, Joe. Well, don't wonder.

JOE: I guess the big problem wouldn't be the drowning as much as the boredom, huh?

COLLINS: See you, Joe.

JOE: Night, Mr. Collins.

Scene 19
Arcana

STAN *and* JOE *walk across the fantail.*

STAN: There are many things in this world, Joe, the true meaning of which we will never know. *(Pause.)* I knew a man was a Mason . . .

JOE: Uh huh . . .

STAN: You know what he told me?

JOE: No.

Pause.

STAN: Would you like to know?

JOE: Yes.

As STAN *starts to speak, they continue around the fantail and out of sight.*

Scene 20
Dolomite

COLLINS *continues to the bridge.* SKIPPY *is in command of the ship.* COLLINS *philosophizes.*

COLLINS *(to* SKIPPY*):* You know, it's surprising what people will convince themselves is interesting. The Company, guests come on for a trip and we're docked at Port Arthur and they're up on the boatdeck and for an hour, an hour and a half, they're watching this stuff pour into the holds. Just watching it pour into the holds and the dust is flying and it's hard to breathe. But they're just standing there. The woman's got a Brownie. She's taking pictures of rock falling off a conveyor belt. Now what is so interesting about that? I'd like to know. If you described the situation to them, to any normal people, they wouldn't walk across the hall to watch it if the TV were broken. But there they are, guests of the Company. Standing there on the boatdeck hours on end, watching the rocks and the dust. Maybe they see something I don't. Maybe I'm getting jaded.

Pause.

What are they looking at?

SKIPPY: What are *you* looking at? You're looking at them.

COLLINS: That's perfectly correct.

SKIPPY: It's all a matter of perspective. *(Pause.)* *Yes*sir. *(Pause.)*

Scene 21
The Bridge

SKIPPY *is alone as* COLLINS *leaves the bridge.* JOE *and* DALE *are alone in the galley.*

SKIPPY *(on the radio):* W.A.Y., Chicago, this is the *T. Harrison,* Harrison Steel, en route. I am ready to copy. Over.

JOE: What time you go off?

DALE: Around six-thirty.

JOE: Hit the bridge before then.

DALE: Yeah.

JOE: Hit it in about a half-hour.

DALE: Yeah.

JOE: Hit it about six. You made up the First's cabin yet?

DALE: Yeah. I was up forward a little while ago. Going to be a nice day.

JOE: Hot.

DALE: You think?

JOE: Yeah. Well, be hot when we tie up. Be hot before we hit the Soo. You going up the street?

DALE: Oh, I don't know. Later maybe. Going to get some sleep first.

JOE: They got some nice bars up there.

DALE: Yeah?

JOE: Oh yeah. I know. Got some real bars up there. Sedate . . . Yeah. I used to go up there. To go drinking up there.

DALE: You off now?

JOE: Naw. I don't go off till the eight o'clock come on. I don't go off till eight.

DALE: You hungry?

JOE: Yeah, a little.

DALE: Want me to fix you something?

JOE: Naw. I'll get me some pie, something. We got any pie left?

DALE: Should be some. Want something to drink? A glass of milk?

JOE: Naw, I'll just get some coffee. You know, Dale . . . you go to school?

DALE: Yeah, I'm in my second year.

JOE: You're starting your second year, you finished one year?

DALE: Yeah. I'll be starting my sophomore year in September. When I go back.

JOE: Where do you go at?

DALE: In Massachusetts. Near Boston.

JOE: What do you go all the way there for?

DALE: Well, I like it there. It's a good school. . . . It's a nice area.

JOE: Yeah, but they got good schools over here, don't they? I mean, I'm sure it's a good place . . . where you go. But they got good schools here, too. Loyola, Chicago University, some good schools here . . . Michigan.

DALE: Oh, yeah. They're good schools. But I like it in the East.

JOE: It's nice there, huh?

DALE: Yes, very nice. Nice country. I like it there.

JOE: What are you studying, I mean, what do you work at, at school?

DALE: I'm studying English. English Literature.

JOE: Yeah? That's a tough racket. I mean, writing. But . . . what? Are you gonna teach? To teach English?

DALE: Oh, I don't know. I'm just . . . studying it because I like it.

JOE: Yeah.

DALE: I may teach.

JOE: Sure, I mean . . . all I mean, it's a tough racket, you know? . . . Hitting the bridge soon?

DALE: Yup.

JOE: How long will you be staying on the boat? About?

DALE: Oh, I don't know. Another month, five weeks.

JOE: Got to go back to school, back East, huh?

DALE: Yeah. I'll leave to go back to school.

JOE: Want a cup? . . . Going back to your studies. Back East. I used to go East. I worked out of Buffalo for a while. I shipped Ford out of Detroit, too. Ford Boats. Ever shipped salt?

DALE: No, you?

JOE: Never did. Always wanted to, though. It's a different life, you know?

DALE: Yeah.

JOE: It must be nice out there. Be pretty easy to ship out. Out of Chicago. I'm an A.B., did you know that? . . . You should get out of Stewards, you know? Get on the deck, get rid of this straight-shift crap. If you were on the deck we could go up street at Duluth, Arthur. You'd be out, free, until four in the afternoon and you'd be free at eight and we could fuck around all night, you know? Really hit the bars.

DALE: It's not so bad, really. I have my days free, I get some sun.

JOE: Yeah, but it's not the same thing, it's like having a *job*, for crissakes. I mean, it's okay if you like it.

DALE: It's all right.

JOE: I been working on the Lakes off and on for twenty-three years. It don't seem like such a long time. How old are you, Dale, if you don't mind my asking?

DALE: No, I'm eighteen. Be nineteen in October.

JOE: Yeah? You're a young guy for such a . . . I mean, you're not that *young* but you seem . . . older, you know? You seem like you wouldn't of been that young. Of course, that's not that young. I was working on the boats before I was your age. I'm going to get some more pie. . . . You can see the bridge. You can just make it out. Like a landmark out there. You know, that is one pretty bridge. We been going under that bridge for once or twice a week since I was your age off and on, but that sure is a pretty bridge.

DALE: Yeah, I like it.

JOE: But, I mean, what the fuck? It's a bridge, right? It's something that you use and takes cars from over there over to the island. They don't let no cars drive on that island, did you know that? It's a law. But what I mean, you usually do not think about things that way. From that standpoint. But when you look at it . . . it's just a bridge to get people from the island over to there on the beach . . . you know what I mean.

DALE: Yeah.

JOE: And . . . you go underneath of it and look up and all the same it's pretty. And you forget that it *does* something. But this beauty of it makes what it does all the more . . . nice. Do you know what I'm talking about?

DALE: Yeah, Joe.

JOE: Sometimes I get . . . well, I don't express myself too well, I guess.

DALE: No, I know what you mean.

JOE: You know, you got it made, Dale. You know that? You really got it made.

DALE: What do you mean?

JOE: You got your whole life ahead of you. I mean, you're not a *kid* or anything . . . you're a man. You're a young man. But you got it made.

DALE: What are you talking about, Joe?

JOE: Ah, you know what I'm saying.

DALE: You're not an old man, Joe. What are you talking about?

JOE: Ah, you know what I'm saying to you. I just wanted to tell you, Dale. I just wanted to let you know. So you'll understand. I mean. I've lived longer than you have. And at this stage one can see a lot of things in their proper light. And . . . you're a bright kid.

DALE: Well, sometimes I don't think so.

JOE: Well, what do you know? You know? I mean I've lived a hell of a lot longer than you have and I want to tell you, you're going to be Okay. You're a fine, good-looking kid and you know what's happening. You're okay and you're a good worker. . . . I don't mean that disrespectfully.

DALE: . . . I know.

JOE: And I just want to tell you, sincerely, you have got it made.

DALE: Well.

JOE: No, it's the truth. Christ it's going to be hot today. Going to be a hell of a hot fucking day. Did you make up the First's cabin today?

DALE: Before you came in.

JOE: You don't have take no shit from him, you know.

DALE: I know that.

JOE: He give you any trouble?

DALE: No, not at all.

JOE: Well, you don't have to take nothing from him. You just do your job. And if he gives you any trouble you talk to the Union Rep when we hit the beach. You know? You just do a good job . . . because that's what he's there for.

DALE: Okay.

JOE: I mean it. If he gives you shit, just let me know.

DALE: Okay, Joe. I'll do that.

JOE: Seriously. We should raise Mackinaw in a couple of minutes. You going up on deck?

DALE: No, I gotta finish up here.

JOE: Yeah, well, I'll see you later. Let me know if you're going up the street, huh?

DALE: I will, Joe.

JOE: We'll hit the bars.

DALE: I will.

JOE: You drink?

Pause.

DALE: Yeah.

JOE: Well, I'm going up on the boatdeck. You get off soon, huh?

DALE: In about a half-hour.

JOE: Well, take it easy, Dale. Get some rest. Can you sleep in this heat?

DALE: Easy. I got a scoop out the porthole.

JOE: Oh. Well, it's just that I have trouble sometimes. Well, take it easy, kid.

DALE: Don't work too hard.

JOE: Fuck no. I wouldn't.

Scene 22
Fast Examined

STAN, *on the main deck, buttonholes* COLLINS.

STAN: . . . at least eight. But he doesn't ever draw his gun. He's giving 'em one of these (whack) and a couple of these, and some of these, twisting and like a ballet. Till there's one left. Behind the bar. And all you see: Jonnie's got his back to the bar. We think he thinks this guy is dead. And you see the guy take this cleaver off the bar and heft it over his head and just as he starts to let go, Fast whips around and fires. (Carries this belly pistol. Black as night. In his *sleeve,* in his fucking sleeve.) He goes whomp, like that, and the fucking thing slides down his sleeve and into his hand. And you see the guy's still got his hand up to throw but all you see is this little bit of bloody handle. Fast shot the cleaver out of the guy's fucking hand. BE-HIND HIS BACK. Twenty, thirty feet with a two-inch belly pistol. Now, how stark is that?

Scene 23
The .38

In the engine room.

FIREMAN: . . . a big black Colt's revolver. A .38 or a .44. Pure blue-black with a black checker grips and an eyelet on the butt for a lanyard—it was an old gun, but in good shape. No scratches. Purest black as a good pair of boots. Must've been re-blued. Or maybe he never used it. You don't know. Used big shells, powerful. You could tell from how big they were. That's a good way to tell. I was in the Army. Overseas. Hawaii. But it wasn't a state. The officers had pistols. They were automatic. .45's. Big heavy things. But his was a revolver. I've seen it. Shit, he used to take it down here to clean it. He worked down here a while. Don't know how they ever took him. A big guy as quick as he was. I don't see how. Unless they drugged him—or took him from behind.

FRED: I heard they might have drugged him.

FIREMAN: Bastards.

FRED: Or he was drunk.

FIREMAN: Possible. Possible. Very possible. That boy drank. Used to drink on the ship.

FRED: Who doesn't?

FIREMAN: Not him, not him, for sure. No sir, stagger around like an Indian when he had a few. Like a goddamn Winnebago Indian he would.

FRED: That's probably what happened. Did he have his gun with him?

FIREMAN: What'd you hear?

FRED: Did't hear one way or the other.

FIREMAN: The way I hear it . . . he *took* it. He took the gun to the bar . . . but when they *found* him. HE DIDN'T HAVE IT ON HIM.

FRED: Huh?

FIREMAN: He was a mysterious fellow.

FRED: Huh?

FIREMAN: But he had a lot of gumption.

FRED: I heard that, I didn't know him.

FIREMAN: Yup, a lot of gall.

FRED: Oh yeah.

FIREMAN: I hated that . . . young fellow, what does he know? Blind balls is all. Damn fool like to get killed. Crazy. Crazy, is all. With a big gun like that.

FRED: Maybe he didn't have it on him.

FIREMAN: He had it. I think he had it, by God. I saw him going off and I said to myself, "He looks like trouble. He just is dripping trouble today. I hope he's got his piece. I just hope, for his own sake that he's got it."

FRED: The cops would know if he had it.

FIREMAN: Or someone could have looked in his stuff.

FRED: They cleaned it out, huh?

FIREMAN: Yeah, been cleaned out. I'd say, for sure. The Mate's responsible.

FRED: Well, whether he took it or not, they got him.

FIREMAN: Fucking cops.

FRED: Yeah . . . why do you say "cops"?

FIREMAN: You kidding? It was the cops got him. Or Uncle Sam.

FRED: The G? What'd the G want with Guiglialli?

FIREMAN: You kidding? With what that kid knew?

FRED: What'd he know?

FIREMAN: Things. He knew things.

FRED: Yeah?

FIREMAN: Surer'n hell, that kid. He'd let on like he didn't know, but he knew. I know when they know. I can see it. And that kid's been around. The cops, they don't like that they find out, they don't sit still. They know. That kid was no cherry, either. He was no dumb kid. I think he was on the run. I think they wanted him.

FRED: The Coast Guard wouldn't let him on the boats if he was wanted. They print you. You know that.

FIREMAN: Still . . .

FRED: How could he get on?

FIREMAN: He had friends. That kid had friends, I tell you. Politics. Strings. You don't know one-half of what he knew. He was no cheap talker, that kid. Talk is cheap.

FRED: You think it was the G, huh?

FIREMAN: I think what I think. That's all I know.

Scene 24
Subterfuge

DALE *is at work in the galley.* JOE *comes in.*

JOE: Hey, Dale. I heard the Steward's in charge of First Aid.

DALE: What's the matter?

JOE: It's just that I heard that. Is it the truth?

DALE: Yup.

JOE: Good. Good. I heard that. What I wanted to know and was wondering, out of curiosity, is: What happens if a guy gets his leg chopped off and they have to give him something. What do they give him?

DALE: Morphine, I guess.

JOE: They keep that stuff on the ship here?

DALE: Not as far as I know. You'd have to ask the Steward.

JOE: Oh, I wouldn't want to have to do that, because I'm just curious. I didn't really want to *know* or anything, you know?

DALE: I understand.

JOE: The Steward's the only one's got keys to First Aid, huh?

DALE: Right.

JOE: Well, all right. Thanks, you know.

Pause.

But would you do me a favor?

DALE: Sure.

JOE: Would you get me a couple of aspirins and a glass of water?

DALE: Sure, Joe. You got a headache?

JOE: Yeah. I'm not feeling so good the last couple of days.

DALE: What is it?

JOE: I don't know. My back down near my kidneys. It hurts. My head hurts all the time, you know?

DALE: You think it's serious?

JOE: I don't know. It just hurts. It makes you feel old, you know? Sometimes you just get so sick of everything, nothing seems any good, you know? It's all you—don't care . . . Ahhh, it's just me being sick, is all.

DALE: I thought you didn't look right today.

JOE: My hair hurts.

DALE: Mmmmm.

JOE: And my kidney hurts when I walk—I think I'm dying.

DALE: You don't look like you're dying, Joe.

JOE: I sure as hell feel like I am. Sheeeeit.

DALE: Just try to think it won't always be like this, Joe. It's just a temporary illness, in a day or two or a week it'll be all over.

JOE: That's easy for you to say. You don't know what I got.

DALE: What have you got?

JOE: I don't know.

DALE: Well. You can see a doctor the next time we tie up.

JOE: Yeah. It kinda frightens me.

DALE: It does?

JOE: I don't wanna almost find out what I got.

DALE: It's probably nothing serious, Joe. A virus, a little flu or some inflammation, you know?

JOE: Or infection.

DALE: A little infection isn't going to hurt you, Joe. It might only be a touch of stomach flu, something that's going to be over in a day or two. Have you had fever?

JOE: Yeah. At night I been sweating out the sheets terrible. It's inhuman to sleep in them, you know? And I get cold, I don't know. I'm so fucking sick of being sick.

DALE: How long has it been? Four or five days?

JOE: Off and on, yeah, and longer than that.

DALE: You should see a doctor, Joe.

Scene 25
Fingers

JOE *wanders off.* DALE *goes on deck for a cigarette and encounters* FRED *at work.*

FRED: Collucci lost two fingers in the winch.

DALE: Which winch?

FRED: Forward main.

DALE: Who's Collucci?

FRED: Used to ship deck.

DALE: When did he lose them?

FRED: This was a couple, four—five years.

DALE: Yeah.

FRED: He got thirty-six hundred bucks.

DALE: The Company paid him?

FRED: Not counting Workman's Comp and Social Security.

DALE: Do you get Social Security for fingers?

FRED: I don't know. But not counting it he got thirty-six hundred bucks. Eighteen hundred bucks a finger.

DALE: The main winch? Which fingers?

FRED: Right hand. These two.

DALE: That's a bitch. He's crippled.

FRED: Two fingers?

DALE: But the thumb.

FRED: What about it, for thirty-six hundred?

DALE: How could he pick anything up?

FRED: Used the other fucking hand. If they paid him five bucks every time he wanted to pick something up just to use his left hand he'd get . . . thirty-six hundred bucks. . . . For 720 times . . . That's not so much.

DALE: I wouldn't do it.

FRED: He didn't do it on purpose.

DALE: I wouldn't do it at all. Even by accident. No amount of money.

FRED: I think.

DALE: You can't buy a finger, man. It's gone and that's it. Not for all the money in the world.

FRED: Yeah, neither would I.

SKIPPY *and* COLLINS, *on the bridge, are overheard.*

SKIPPY: . . . explain it when we don't make schedule on this watch, you.

COLLINS: I called ahead. They'll have the mail right at the lock.

Scene 26
Joe's Suicide

DALE, *off watch, is sharing a beer with* JOE *on the boatdeck.*

JOE: You get paid for doing a job. You trade the work for money, am I right? Why is it any fucking less good than being a doctor, for example? That's one thing I never wanted to be, a doctor. I used to want to be lots of things when I was little. You know, like a kid. I wanted to be a ballplayer like everyone. And I wanted to be a cop, what does a kid know, right? And can I tell you something that I wanted to be? I know this is going to sound peculiar, but it was a pure desire on my part. One thing I wanted to be when I was little (I don't mean to be bragging now, or just saying it). If you were there you would have known, it was a pure desire on my part. I wanted to be a dancer. That's one thing I guard. Like you might guard the first time you got laid, or being in love with a girl. Or winning a bike at the movies . . . well, maybe not that. More like getting married, or winning a medal in the war. I wanted to be a dancer. Not tap, I mean a real ballet dancer. I know they're all fags, but I didn't think about it. I didn't *not* think about it. That is, I didn't say, "I want to be a dancer but I do *not* want to be a fag." It just wasn't important. I saw myself arriving at the theater late doing Swan Lake at the Lyric Opera. With a coat with one of those old-time collars. (It was winter.) And on stage with a purple shirt and white tights catching these girls . . . beautiful light girls. Sweating. All my muscles are covered in sweat. you know? But it's clean. And my muscles all feel tight. Every fucking muscle in my body. Hundreds of them. Tight and working. And I'm standing up straight on stage with this kind of expression on my face waiting to catch this girl. I was about fifteen. It takes a hell of a lot of work to be a dancer. But a dancer doesn't even fucking care if he is somebody. He *is* somebody so much so it's not important. You know what I mean? Like these passengers we get. Guests of the Company. Always being important. If they're so fucking important, who gives a fuck? If they're really important why the fuck do they got to tell you about it?

DALE: I remember in a journalism class in high school the teacher used to say, never use the word famous in a story. Like "Mr. X, famous young doctor . . ."

JOE: Right, because if they're fucking famous, why do you have to say it?

DALE: And he said if they're *not* . . .

JOE: Then what the fuck are you saying it for, right?

DALE: Right.

JOE: It's so fucking obvious you could puke. No class cocksuckers. You ever try to . . . I don't want to get you offended by this, you don't have to answer it if you don't want to.

DALE: No, go ahead.

JOE: I mean, what the fuck? If you're going to talk to somebody, why fuck around the bush, right? Did you ever try to kill yourself?

DALE: No.

JOE: I did one time. I should say that perhaps I shouldn't say I "tried" to kill myself, meaning the gun didn't work. But I wanted to.

DALE: Yeah.

JOE: I had this gun when I lived over on the South Side. I won it in a poker game.

DALE: Yeah.

JOE: Aaaaaaah, I fucking bought it off the bumboat in Duluth. Why lie? Forty bucks. A revolver. .32 revolver. Six shots, you know?

DALE: How big a barrel?

JOE: A couple of inches. Like this. I never fired it. One time, coming back, I loaded it and fired one shot off the fantail into the water. I didn't hit anything. I used to clean it. Got this kit in the mail. Patches and oil and gunslick and powder solvent and this brush.

DALE: I've seen them.

JOE: I kept it in my suitcase. One night in Gary, I had this apartment. I was cleaning my gun and, you know how you do, pretending the cops were after me and doing fast draws in the mirror.

DALE: Yeah.

JOE: And I said, "What am I doing? A grown man playing bang bang with a gun in some fucking dive in Gary Indiana at ten o'clock at night?" And I lay down in front of the TV and loaded the gun. Five chambers. You shouldn't load the sixth in case you jiggle on your horse and blow your foot off.

DALE: Yeah.

JOE: And I put the end in my mouth, and I couldn't swallow and I could feel my pulse start to beat and my balls contract and draw up. You ever feel that?

DALE: No.

JOE: And I took it out of my mouth and laid down on

the bed on my back and looked at the ceiling and put the gun under my chin pointing at my brain. But after a while I started feeling really stupid. And I rolled over and put the gun under my pillow, but I still held onto it. And I started. You know, playing with myself, you know what I mean.

DALE: I know.

JOE: A grown man, isn't that something?

Scene 27
Collins and Skippy on the Bridge

> COLLINS *has been in control of the boat.* SKIPPY *comes on the bridge.*

SKIPPY: Yo, Mr. Collins.

COLLINS: Yessir.

SKIPPY We pick up the mail?

COLLINS: Yes *sir.*

SKIPPY Good.

COLLINS: We got that report on Guiliani.

SKIPPY That's fine. Get me something to eat.

COLLINS: Yessir. *(Spotting* JOE) Yo, Litko!

JOE: Yo . . . !

Scene 28
In the Galley

FRED: I don't give a fuck; the man lived on the sea, the man *died* on the sea.

DALE: He died on land.

FRED: He died 'cause *of* the sea. 'Cause of the sea. 'Cause of his *trade*. You understand?

DALE: Yeah.

FRED: Good.

> *Pause.*

DALE: He died 'cause of his desires.

> *Pause.*

FRED: Yeah.

> *Pause.*

Well, we all *have* 'em. . . .

Pause.

DALE: You know him well?

FRED: I knew him *very* well, Dale, *very* well.

JOE *enters the galley.*

Yo, Joe. . . !

JOE: Yo, Fred.

FRED: I'm telling my man about Guiliani.

JOE: Yeah. They called the ship. We're picking him up in Duluth.

FRED: We're picking *who* up?

JOE: What?

FRED: *Who* we're picking up?

JOE: Guigliani.

FRED: We're picking up Guigliani?

JOE: Yeah. He caught the train.

FRED: He caught the train to Duluth?

JOE: Yeah.

Pause.

FRED: How come he missed the boat?

JOE: Yeah. Skippy said he said his aunt died, but he thinks the *real* reason 'cause he overslept.

FRED: . . . sonofabitch . . .

JOE: Well, I'll be glad to have him back.

FRED: *Oh* yeah . . .

DALE: You want a cup of coffee?

JOE: Thank you.

COLLINS, *on the bridge, is seen talking into the ship-to-shore radio.*

COLLINS: W.A.Y. Chicago, this is the *T. Harrison* en route.

Pause.

I read you five-by-five.